DONALD WELLS

# Learn English Through Stories

*16 Stories to Improve Your English Grammar and English Vocabulary*

# Contents

# 1

# Introduction

Are you trying to improve your English? This book can help you develop your understanding of English grammar and vocabulary in a natural and effective way—through stories. It has 16 short, easy-to-understand stories which you can use to test and improve your English. Each story is presented in three versions: Basic English, Intermediate English, and Advanced English.

The Basic English version of each story uses simple grammar and vocabulary. Sentences use very minimal verb conjugation, ordinary vocabulary, and shorter structures for ease of understanding. By understanding the basic ideas of the story in this way, readers can then follow the story more easily as the complexity of the grammar and vocabulary increases.

The Intermediate English version introduces different verb tenses and more complex vocabulary and grammatical structures. The basics of the story, however, will remain the same. Some English learners who are operating at a higher level might want to begin with the Intermediate English version of each story. Choose the version which seems best for your own language level.

Finally, the Advanced English version presents the story at the level of a native English speaker. This version will provide English learners with the biggest challenge—but because the story is still the same, it should still be easy to follow. In fact, learners can expand their vocabulary and their understanding of grammar in this way!

A set of ten study questions follows the Advanced English version of each story. Use these questions to self-check your understanding of new vocabulary words and your story comprehension. Answers and explanations can be found after each set of ten questions.

By the end of this book, you will have a better, more intuitive understanding of how English works. Just read the stories, try to answer the questions, and check your answers. For extra practice, you can try to translate different versions of the stories into your native language. I recommend using the Intermediate English or Advanced English versions for this purpose, since the Basic English may be too simple for a comfortable translation.

All the stories used in this book have been adapted from Aesop's fables. These are ancient stories attributed to the Greek writer Aesop which were meant to teach basic moral lessons. The lessons are given at the end of the Advanced English version of each story in a short sentence introducing the Moral.

2

# Contents

# 3

# The Boy Who Cried Wolf

<u>Basic English</u>

There is a boy who lives in a small village. He likes to make jokes and tell lies. One day, he tells everyone in the village that there is a wolf just outside in the woods. Everyone is afraid for their children. The men get together and go look for the wolf. They find nothing. The boy laughs to himself about how upset everyone in the village is.

Later, he does it again. He warns everyone about the wolf. Everyone is scared. They stop working and go look for the wolf. Again, they find nothing. This time, the people become angry with the boy for lying to them.

Then one day the boy really does see a wolf. The wolf chases him. He runs into the village and cries for help. But no one comes to see. They do not believe any wolf is there. So, the wolf catches and eats the boy.

<u>Intermediate English</u>

There once was a boy who lived in a small village. He liked to make jokes and tell lies. One day, he told everyone in the village that he saw a wolf in the nearby forest. The villagers got scared, and parents worried for the safety of their children. The men of the village banded together to go find and kill the wolf. But they didn't find anything, because it was all a lie. The boy just laughed and laughed to himself about how upset he had made everyone.

A week later, he tried it again. He told everyone in the village about a great big, grey wolf he had just seen. Just as before, everyone became worried and the men gathered and searched for the wolf. Again, they found nothing. This time, though, the people of the village realized the lie and became very angry with the boy.

As it happened, one day the boy went out walking in the woods and he really did see a wolf. The wolf chased him back to the village, where he cried out for someone to come save him. But no one came out to see or even looked up from their work. They no longer believed the boy or his lies about wolves. And so, the wolf caught the boy and ate him up.

## Advanced English

Once upon a time, there was a boy who lived in a small village. He was a mischievous sort who liked to joke and tell lies. One day, he got the idea of lying about having seen a wolf in the nearby forest. The villagers believed his story and immediately began to worry for the safety of themselves and their children. The men of the village banded together to search for the wolf and kill it if they could. But of course, they didn't find anything. Meanwhile, the boy just laughed and laughed at them. The sight of everyone running around with such concern on their faces delighted him to no end.

A week later, he tried the same trick again. "There's a gigantic grey wolf on the outskirts of town," he shouted. Again, everyone was worried. The men of the village conducted a thorough search of the nearby forest and concluded that the boy had lied to them again. Realizing they had been duped, the villagers became quite angry with the boy.

As it happened, the boy was playing around in the forest some time after this when he really did see a wolf. What's worse, the wolf saw him. The boy raced back to the village as fast as he could go, with the wolf getting closer and closer at every step. "The wolf is here," he cried out, "he's after me!" But this time, no one in the village stopped working or bothered to check on the boy. "Another one of his tales," they said to themselves. And so, instead of being saved, the boy was caught by the wolf—who tore him limb from limb and ate him up.

## Moral

A liar is not believed, even when he tells the truth.

## 10 Study Questions

(answers and explanations are below)

1) Mischievous most nearly means
   a) angry
   b) naughty
   c) disturbing
   d) scandalous

2) Band together most nearly means
   a) play together
   b) work carefully
   c) combine forces
   d) help each other

3) Thorough most nearly means
   a) difficult
   b) sudden
   c) powerful
   d) complete

4) Duped most nearly means
   a) stupid
   d) wrong
   c) difficult
   d) deceived

5) Bother most nearly means
   a) forget
   b) accept

c) think about

d) spend effort

6) How did the boy respond when the villagers got upset by his lies?

7) What did the men of the village do to try to get rid of the wolf?

8) The second time the boy told a lie something different happened. What was it?

9) Why didn't the villagers rescue the boy from the wolf at the end?

10) How does the story show the moral?

## Answers and Explanations

1) Mischievous most nearly means NAUGHTY (b). Mischievous is an adjective meaning a person or animal who seems fond of causing harm or trouble. Naughty is the best match because naughty means badly behaved.

2) Band together most nearly means COMBINE FORCES (c). Band together is a phrasal verb meaning to join up in a single unit, usually with the idea of improving effectiveness. "Combine forces" is another way of expressing this idea.

3) Thorough most nearly means COMPLETE (d). Thorough is an adjective that means complete in every detail or performed with great care and completeness. The idea of being "complete" is part of the meaning of this word.

4) Duped most nearly means DECEIVED (d). To dupe someone means to trick them, and to be duped means to be tricked or deceived. To deceive means to cause someone to believe something that isn't true. These two

words are more closely related than the other words.

5) Bother most nearly means SPEND EFFORT (d). To bother means to take the time or the trouble to do something. This is another way of saying to "spend effort" on doing something. In the story, "no one in the village… bothered to check on the boy" means that no one spent any effort on him.

6) The boy responded in two ways: He laughed at the villagers. ("The boy just laughed and laughed at them.") And he was delighted by their reaction. ("The sight of everyone… delighted him to no end.")

7) The men banded together. They searched for the wolf. They tried to find and kill the wolf. ("The men of the village banded together to search for the wolf and kill it if they could.")

8) The second time he told a lie, the villagers realized the trick and became angry with him. ("Realizing they had been duped, the villagers became quite angry with the boy.")

9) The villagers didn't rescue him because they didn't believe him. ("Another one of his tales, they said to themselves.") And they didn't stop what they were doing to check on him. ("But this time, no one in the village stopped working or bothered to check on the boy.")

10) The villagers realize the boy is lying. As a result, even though he is telling the truth at the end, no one believes him because of the lies he told in the past. ("But this time… And so, instead of being saved the boy was caught by the wolf.") Since the result is the boy's death, the moral is shown quite strongly.

# 4

# The Sour Grapes

### Basic English

One day a Fox sees a beautiful bunch of grapes. The grapes hang on a vine in a tree. The grapes seem ready to burst with juice because they are so ripe. The fox feels his mouth water as he looks at the grapes longingly.

Since the grapes are so high off the ground, the Fox must jump up to reach them. He tries it but misses badly. He walks off a short distance and takes a running jump at the grapes, but again he falls short. Again and again he tries, but each time he falls short.

Finally, he sits down and looks up at the grapes with disgust. It is foolish to waste time and the grapes are probably sour anyway. With these thoughts in mind, he walks away from the tree in contempt.

### Intermediate English

One day there was a Fox who saw a beautiful bunch of ripe grapes. The grapes were hanging on a vine twisted around a tree branch. The grapes seemed ready to burst with juice due to their ripeness. The Fox's mouth started watering as he gazed at the grapes longingly.

The grapevine was so high, the Fox had to jump up to have any chance of reaching them. He tried but fell well short of the mark. So, he walked off a short way and took a good running jump at the grapes. Unfortunately, he fell short yet again. Over and over he tried, but it was no use. He simply couldn't reach those grapes.

Finally, he sat down and looked up at the grapes in disgust. All he could think of is what a fool he was to waste his efforts this way on a bunch of grapes which were probably sour anyway. With these thoughts in mind, he walked away from the tree in contempt.

## Advanced English

One day there was a Fox who spotted an attractive bunch of grapes hanging from a vine. The vine was carefully trained along the branches of a tree, and its grapes were so ripe they seemed ready to burst with their juices. Just looking at them made the Fox's mouth water.

Since the vine was pretty high up, he had to jump to have any hope of reaching the grapes. The first time he tried this, he fell well short of the mark. So, he took a good running jump at the grapes. Try as he might, however, the Fox simply couldn't close the distance between himself and his delicious prize.

Finally, realizing it was no use, he sat down and looked at the grapes with disgust. "What a fool I am," he chided himself. "I've been wasting my time on a bunch of grapes that are probably sour anyway!" And with that, he stalked off scornfully.

## Moral

Many pretend to despise and belittle things which are beyond their reach.

## 10 Study Questions
(answers and explanations are below)

1) Trained most nearly means
   a) sent
   b) hung
   c) directed
   d) constructed

2) Burst most nearly means
  a) destroy
  b) explode
  c) intensify
  d) demonstrate

3) Fall short most nearly means
  a) miss
  b) delay
  c) sense
  d) forget

4) Chide most nearly means
  a) deny
  b) blame
  c) abstain
  d) concentrate

5) Scornfully most nearly means
  a) quietly
  b) carefully
  c) completely
  d) disdainfully

6) What is the relationship between these items: grapes, vine, tree?

7) Why does the fox want the grapes?

8) What does he do to try to reach the grapes?

9) Why does the fox stop trying to get the grapes?

10) How does the story show the moral?

## Answers and Explanations

1) Trained most nearly means DIRECTED (c). Plants which have been *trained* have been made to grow in a certain direction or in a particular way.

2) Burst most nearly means EXPLODE (b). To burst is when a container breaks apart suddenly, spilling its contents (either due to an impact or some internal pressure). In the story, the grapes are so full of juice they are about ready to explode, which is another way of saying to break forth suddenly.

3) Fall short most nearly means MISS (a). Fall short is a phrasal verb meaning to fail to reach something. It can mean something abstract like a goal or a standard, or it can mean something physical like in the story where the fox cannot physically reach the grapes.

4) Chide most nearly means BLAME (b). To chide someone (or oneself) means to scold, rebuke, or blame someone (or oneself). Typically, one would "chide oneself" for foolish behavior—as the fox does in this story.

5) Scornfully most nearly means DISDAINFULLY (d). Scorn is a feeling that someone or something is worthless or contemptible. It is a feeling of disdain for something. The adverb form 'scornfully' means to act in this manner.

6) The relationship between the three items is this: the grapes hang on the vine and the vine is itself twisted along the branches of a tree. The grapes are on the vine, which is on the tree.

7) The fox wants the grapes because they seem so delicious. The grapes are described as "attractive," and they make the fox's mouth "water" (which means the saliva comes up in his mouth in anticipation of eating something).

8) The fox jumps up and then tries to take a "running jump" to reach the grapes.

9) He stops because he is unable to reach them and decides that it is "no use" (which means that he will not be able to reach the grapes no matter what he does).

10) The grapes are beyond the fox's reach, so he says that they are "probably sour anyway." It is unlikely that the grapes are sour, but instead the fox tells himself that they are sour to make his inability to reach them more acceptable to himself.

# 5

## The Wolf or the Eagle

### Basic English

A flock of goats lives on the side of a mountain. There is an Eagle who lives high above them. One day he gets hungry and attacks one of the goats. He kills and eats the goat and finds it delicious. Every day for the next week he kills and eats another goat.

Finally, the goats get together to decide what to do about their problem. One of the goats suggests that they go into the valley and ask the Wolf to protect them. The Wolf is unwilling at first, but the goats are so determined that he agrees.

The next day, the Eagle comes for his meal and the Wolf surprises him. The Wolf attacks and hurts the Eagle so badly that the Eagle decides to make his home on another mountain. But when the goats gather to thank the wolf for his work, the Wolf tells them he is hungry, and in one day he kills and eats 20 of the flock: far more than the Eagle.

### Intermediate English

There once was a flock of goats living on the side of a mountain with an Eagle living high on the mountain above them. One day the Eagle started feeling hungry, and he decided to try out some goat meat for a change. He killed and ate one of the goats and found it delicious. Every day for the next week, he dined on another goat.

After a time, the goats got together to decide what they should do about their problem. One of them suggested that they go into the valley and ask the Wolf to protect them. At first, the Wolf was unwilling to lend his services, but the goats convinced him at last that he was strong enough to defend them from the Eagle.

The next day, when the Eagle came for his meal, the Wolf surprised him. In the attack, the Eagle was so badly injured that he decided to move his home to another mountain. But when the goats gathered to thank the Wolf for his efforts, the Wolf took one look at them and began licking his lips. Before they could do anything, he had fallen upon them, and in one day he had eaten up 20 of them—far more than what the Eagle had ever done.

## Advanced English

There once was a flock of goats living on the side of a mountain. High above them in his eyrie a broad-winged eagle made his home. For some time, they lived together in peace until one day the Eagle got it into his head to try some goat meat for a change. He seized one of them by the neck and snapped it. He made a quick meal of the poor victim and pronounced it delicious. Every day for a week he dined on a different member of the flock.

Seeing no end to the massacre, the goats assembled to debate a course of action. One of them piped up saying, "Let's ask the wolf in the valley to help." At first, the Wolf was unwilling to lend a paw in their defense, but the helpless creatures pleaded so strongly, insisting that only the wolf had the power to stand up to the Eagle, that he began to sense an opportunity.

The next day, when the Eagle came for his meal, the Wolf ambushed him from behind a boulder. In the attack, the Eagle was so badly wounded that he flew away before the wolf could finish him off. "I'll make my home elsewhere," he said as he flew off. "There are other mountains for me to nest on!"

The goats came bounding up to thank the Wolf for saving them, but the Wolf turned on them, baring his fangs. "Did you think I would stop once the Eagle had left?" he asked them. "Now there's nothing standing in my way!" Before any of the flock could respond, he fell upon them left and right—in one afternoon slaughtering dozens more than the Eagle could have managed in a month.

Moral

Avoid a remedy that is worse than the disease.

10 Study Questions

(answers and explanations are below)

1) Eyrie most nearly means
    a) nest
    b) stone
    c) location
    d) mountain

2) Seize most nearly means
    a) kill
    b) drop
    c) grab
    d) change

3) Massacre most nearly means
    a) watch
    b) coverage
    c) placement
    d) destruction

4) Opportunity most nearly means
    a) idea
    b) chance
    c) mistake
    d) difference

5) Ambush most nearly means
  a) jump
  b) attack
  c) vanish
  d) disturb

6) Why does the Eagle start attacking the goats?

7) What do the goats do to save themselves from the Eagle's attacks?

8) What does the Wolf do to the Eagle?

9) What happens to the Eagle?

10) How does the story show the moral?

## Answers and Explanations

1) Eyrie most nearly means NEST (a). An eyrie is a large nest made by a bird of prey like an eagle.

2) Seize most nearly means GRAB (c). To seize something means to take it and hold it, usually suddenly forcibly. Grab also means to take something.

3) Massacre most nearly means DESTRUCTION (d). A massacre is a brutal slaughter or killing. Destruction is the best match for this idea.

4) Opportunity most nearly means CHANCE (b). Opportunity may be defined as a chance to do or accomplish something.

5) Ambush most nearly means ATTACK (b). An ambush is a surprise attack made by someone hidden from the opponent.

LEARN ENGLISH THROUGH STORIES

6) The Eagle has an idea to try to see if goats are tasty: "the Eagle got it into his head to try some goat meat for a change." He eats one of the goats and finds it very tasty indeed.

7) They go to ask the Wolf in the valley to help them. They persuade the Wolf to help.

8) The Wolf ambushes the Eagle and injures him.

9) The Eagle escapes from being killed by the Wolf but decides he will move his home to another mountain.

10) In the story, the goats turn to the Wolf as a "remedy" for the "disease" which is the Eagle's attacks. However, the Wolf in turn does the same thing the Eagle had done, only even more destructive: "in one afternoon slaughtering dozens more than the Eagle could have managed in a month." Therefore, the remedy (the Wolf) is much worse than the disease (the Eagle) had been.

# 6

# The Dog and His Reflection

## Basic English

In town a butcher goes about his work. He cuts up meat to sell to the townsfolk. As he works, a small pile of bones builds up on his table. He sees a little dog nearby and throws one of the bones to the dog. The dog happily grabs the bone and hurries home with the prize as fast as he can go.

As he crosses a small bridge, he looks down and sees his reflection in the water. But the dog believes he sees another dog with another bone—a bone much bigger than his own. He doesn't stop to think about it. Instead, he drops his bone and jumps at the dog he sees in the river. He falls in with a splash, and in a moment, he finds he must swim to shore.

He reaches the shore and looks back at the river sadly. He remembers the good bone he lost and realizes what a foolish dog he is.

## Intermediate English

In town a butcher was going about his work. He was cutting up meat to sell to the townsfolk. As he worked, a small pile of bones built up on the table next to him. He saw a little dog playing nearby and threw one of the bones to the dog. The dog happily grabbed the bone and hurried home with his prize as fast as he could go.

While crossing a small bridge, the dog looked down and saw his reflection in the water. But the dog believed he was seeing another dog with another bone—a bone much bigger than his own. He didn't stop to think about it but instead dropped his bone at once and jumped at the dog he thought he saw. He fell in with a splash only to find himself forced to swim to shore to save his life.

When he reached the shore, he looked back at the river in sadness remembering the good bone he had lost and realizing what a foolish dog he was.

## Advanced English

A town butcher was going about his work one day, cutting up meat to sell to the other townsfolk. As he worked, he steadily built up a small pile of bones on the table next to him. Seeing a dog playing nearby, the butcher decided to be friendly and tossed one of the bones to the dog. The dog gleefully snatched the bone up and hurried home with it as fast as he could go.

While crossing over a small footbridge, however, the dog chanced to see what looked like another dog with a bone much bigger than his own. Of course, the dog was only seeing his own reflection, but in his greed, he didn't stop to think. Instead, he dropped his bone in the river and leapt at his own reflection. He fell into the deep water with a splash, but rather than catch a bone he found himself forced to swim to shore to save his life.

After reaching the shore the dog could only look back at the river mournfully, regretting the good bone he had lost through his folly.

## Moral
It is foolish to be greedy.

## 10 Study Questions
(answers and explanations are below)

1) Toss most nearly means
   a) touch
   b) throw

    c) match

    d) spread

2) Gleefully most nearly means

    a) happily

    b) carefully

    c) mistakenly

    d) disturbingly

3) Reflection most nearly means

    a) bone

    b) image

    c) current

    d) drought

4) Mournfully most nearly means

    a) sadly

    b) kindly

    c) wearily

    d) suddenly

5) Regret most nearly means

    a) contempt

    b) uncertainty

    c) helpfulness

    d) disappointment

6) How does the Dog obtain the bone in the beginning?

7) Where does the Dog see his reflection?

8) Why does the Dog jump into the water?

9) What happens when the Dog jumps in the water?

10) How does the story show the moral?

## Answers and Explanations

1) Toss most nearly means THROW (b). To toss means to throw something lightly, easily, or casually.

2) Gleefully most nearly means HAPPILY (a). Gleefully means in a very joyful manner. Happily is close in meaning to this.

3) Reflection most nearly means IMAGE (b). One of the meanings of reflection (the meaning used in the story here) is an image produced by a mirror or similar surface such as water.

4) Mournfully most nearly means SADLY (a). Mournfully means full or sorrow or sadness.

5) Regret most nearly means DISAPPOINTMENT (d). Regret is a feeling of sadness or disappointment caused by something one has done or not done. In the story, it is disappointment caused by the loss of the Dog's bone.

6) The Dog gets the bone from the town butcher, who throws an extra bone to the Dog as a friendly gesture.

7) The Dog sees his reflection in the river while he is crossing a small bridge.

8) The Dog thinks he is going to "catch a bone" that is "much bigger than his own."

9) The Dog drops his bone in the water and is forced to swim to shore to save his life. He loses his bone and gets wet.

10) The story says "in his greed" to get a bigger bone than the one he has the Dog doesn't stop to consider that he is looking at his reflection rather than a real dog with a real bone. As a result, he does a foolish act which results in losing the bone he has and suffering danger (since he has to swim to shore to save his life). Greed led to foolishness and a regretful result for the Dog.

# 7

# The Chicken and the Fox

One evening a Chicken rests in a tree. As she sits, a Fox comes along and stands at the bottom. He asks if the chicken knows the news. The Chicken says she does not. The Fox explains that all the animals now agree to forget their differences and live together in peace. He asks the Chicken to come down to celebrate with him.

The Chicken agrees to come down, but as she says this she stands up and looks off into the distance. The Fox asks her what it is she sees. She tells him it's a couple of dogs. They must know the good news and want to celebrate.

The Fox does not listen any further. He starts to run off at once. The Chicken asks him why he runs off since the dogs are now his friends. The Fox suspects they do not yet know the news, and besides he has an important errand to run. As he runs away, the Chicken smiles to herself and goes back to sleep.

## Intermediate English
One bright evening a wise old Chicken flew into a tree to rest. As she settled in on her branch, a Fox came along and stood at the bottom. Looking up at her, he asked if she had heard the news yet. Of course, she had not heard, so the Fox explained that the animals had all agreed to forget their differences

and live together in peace and friendship. He encouraged the Chicken to come down to embrace him and celebrate.

While agreeing to come down, the Chicken gazed into the distance as if she could see something approaching. When asked what she was looking at, she replied that it was a couple of dogs. They must also want to celebrate the good news.

Without listening to a word more, the Fox began to run off. The Chicken asked him where he was going since all the animals were friends now, but the Fox only replied that perhaps the dogs had not yet heard the news, and anyway he had a very important errand to run. As the Fox ran off, the Chicken smiled to herself and went back to sleep, grateful to have outwitted a cunning enemy.

## Advanced English

One bright evening as the sun was sinking, a wise old Chicken flew into a tree to roost. But just as she was settling in on her branch, along came a Fox who stood at the bottom of the tree peering up at her. "Have you heard the wonderful news," he cried in a joyful manner. "What news?" she asked. "Your family and mine and all the other animals have agreed to forget their differences and live in peace and friendship together! Isn't it great? Come on down, dear friend, and let us celebrate together."

"How delightful," she replied, but she spoke in an absent-minded way and craned her neck as if looking at something far off in the distance. "What is it you see?" asked the Fox suspiciously. "Why it's only a couple of dogs coming up," she explained. "They must have also heard the good news."

At this, the Fox bounded off at once. "Where are you going?" she called after him. "Oh, perhaps these fellows haven't heard the news," the Fox cried over his shoulder, "and besides, I have an important errand to run that I just remembered!" The Chicken smiled to herself as she buried her head in her feathers and went to sleep, for she had outwitted a crafty adversary.

## Moral
The trickster can also be tricked.

25

## 10 Study Questions
(answers and explanations are below)

1) Roost most nearly means
   a) rest
   b) hang
   c) delay
   d) watch

2) Absent-minded most nearly means
   a) regular
   b) massive
   c) inattentive
   d) celebratory

3) Suspiciously most nearly means
   a) honestly
   b) amusedly
   c) pathetically
   d) distrustfully

4) Bounded off most nearly means
   a) spun out
   b) ran away
   c) closed off
   d) jumped up

5) Adversary most nearly means
   a) student
   b) opponent
   c) consumer
   d) malcontent

6) What time of day does the story take place?

7) What trick does the Fox try to play on the Chicken?

8) How does the Chicken respond to the Fox?

9) Why does the Fox run away?

10) How does the story show the moral?

## Answers and Explanations

1) Roost most nearly means REST (a). Roost means for a bird or cat to settle down to rest of sleep.

2) Absent-minded most nearly means INATTENTIVE (c). Absent-minded means forgetful or inattentive to one's immediate surroundings.

3) Suspiciously most nearly means DISTRUSTFULLY (d). Suspiciously means with careful distrust or suspicion.

4) Bounded off most nearly means RAN AWAY (b). The phrasal verb "bound off" means to bounce away or spring away almost like a ball bouncing off a wall. In the story, the idea is that as soon as the Fox hears that some dogs are approaching, he runs off like a ball bouncing off a wall.

5) Adversary most nearly means OPPONENT (b). An adversary is an opponent in a contest, conflict, or dispute. In the story, the Chicken and the Fox are secret adversaries since the conflict between them is hidden by their clever speeches to each other.

6) The time is sunset because at the beginning of the story it says "as the sun was sinking" (going down).

7) The Fox tries to trick the Chicken into thinking that all the animals have suddenly become friends and thus that he wouldn't be interested in eating her.

8) The Chicken responds by playing her own trick on the Fox. She agrees to come down, but she also pretends that she can see some dogs approaching from a distance.

9) The Fox runs away because the Chicken says some dogs are approaching. The Fox says that maybe the dogs haven't heard the "good news" yet, but most likely he is afraid that the dogs will kill him when they catch him because his "good news" was just a lie.

10) The Fox character is often a trickster, and he begins the story by trying to play a trick on the Chicken. But he is himself tricked by the Chicken, who is probably skeptical of his "wonderful news."

# 8

# The Porcupine and the Snakes

### Basic English

A Porcupine goes to look for a new home. He finds a little cave where a family of Snakes lives. He asks them if he can share their cave with them. The Snakes agree, but they soon regret their decision. Each time one of them turns a corner, it runs into one of the Porcupine's sharp quills.

Tired of the injuries, they politely ask the Porcupine to leave. He replies that he feels quite at home and invites them to leave. To save their skins, the Snakes have no choice but to leave their home and look for another.

### Intermediate English

A Porcupine was looking for a new home one day, when he found a little cave with a family of Snakes living inside it. He asked them if he could share their cave, and they agreed. But soon enough the Snakes came to regret their decision. Whenever one of them tried to move, it seemed, they were constantly running into one of the Porcupine's sharp quills.

They politely asked their unwelcome guest to leave. He merely replied that he felt quite at home now and if anyone had to leave it should be them. To save their skins, the Snakes had no choice but to leave their home and find another.

## Advanced English

Once upon a time there was a Porcupine who went searching for a new home. Presently, he came upon a little cave with a family of Snakes living inside. "Would you mind if I shared your home?" he asked them kindly. The Snakes saw no reason not to have a guest, so they invited him in. Soon enough, they regretted their mistake. The cave was so small that any time a Snake tried to move he found himself getting stuck by one of the Porcupine's sharp quills.

At their wit's end, the Snakes politely asked their unwelcome guest to move on. "I'm very well satisfied where I am, thank you," he replied. "I intend to stay right here." And with that, he firmly escorted the Snakes outdoors and took over their cave for himself. To save their skins, the Snakes had no choice but to find a new home for themselves elsewhere.

## Moral
Give a finger, lose a hand.

## 10 Study Questions
(answers and explanations are below)

1) Unwelcome most nearly means
    a) not helpful
    b) not desired
    c) not present
    d) not capable

2) Save their skins most nearly means
    a) elude capture
    b) contain damage
    c) avoid puncturing
    d) preserve themselves

3) Presently most nearly means

    a) in a specific way
    b) after a short time
    c) at a certain place
    d) with a special feeling

4) At their wit's end most nearly means
    a) unwilling to act
    b) unable to reply
    c) unsure what to do
    d) unaware of the facts

5) Intend most nearly means
    a) plan
    b) need
    c) decide
    d) acclaim

6) What kind of animal is a porcupine?

7) What is the Porcupine looking for at the beginning of the story?

8) Why is it difficult for the Snakes to live with the Porcupine?

9) What happens to the family of Snakes at the end?

10) How does the story show the moral?

## Answers and Explanations

1) Unwelcome most nearly means NOT DESIRED (b). To be welcome is to be desired or invited in somewhere. The prefix un- means NOT this.

2) Save their skins most nearly means PRESERVE THEMSELVES (d). "To

save one's skin" is an idiom meaning to preserve one's life or safety. In the story, the Snakes must abandon their home to the Porcupine to avoid being killed or further injured by him.

3) Presently most nearly means AFTER A SHORT TIME (b). Presently is an adverb meaning "after a short time" or "soon."

4) At their wit's end most nearly means UNSURE WHAT TO DO (c). "To be at wit's end" is an idiom meaning to be so confused that one doesn't know what to do. The idea behind this idiom is that one has reached a point where one's wit (i.e., your mind or your ability to be clever) has no further ideas.

5) Intend most nearly means PLAN (a). Intend means to have a particular course of action in mind, to have a plan.

6) A porcupine is a large rodent about the size of a housecat. Their most notable feature is a coat of long, sharp quills (spines like needles) that covers their bodies. These quills defend the porcupine against predators but can also accidentally stick any animal which happens to get too close. In the story, the porcupine seems to be a rather pushy sort who is willing to throw someone else out of their own house if it suits him.

7) At the beginning of the story, the Porcupine is looking for a home: "there was a Porcupine who went searching for a new home."

8) The difficulty comes from the smallness of the cave and the sharpness of the Porcupine's quills. "The cave was so small that any time a Snake tried to move he found himself getting stuck by one of the Porcupine's sharp quills." The Snakes are constantly getting injured by running into the Porcupine.

9) At the end of the story, the Porcupine throws the Snakes out of their own home and they have to leave and look for a new place to live. The Porcupine "firmly escorted the snakes outdoors and took over their cave for himself," and

the Snakes "had no choice but to find a new home for themselves elsewhere."

10) The moral is "Give a finger, lose a hand." The idea behind this saying is that sometimes when one is generous one ends up losing much more than one intended to give. One meant to give a little (a finger) but ended up losing a lot (the entire hand). In the story, the Snakes give up a little space in their cave to a guest but end up losing the whole cave.

# 9

# The Wolf and the Crane

A Wolf eats too greedily and gets a bone stuck in his throat. He is unable to move it, and with the bone in his throat he is unable to eat. He goes to see a Crane. With her long neck and bill she can easily pull the bone out for him. He promises to reward her if she does.

Although the Crane is nervous, the idea of a reward is pleasing to her. She agrees and quickly pulls out the bone. As soon as she does, the Wolf gets up and walks away. When the Crane asks for her reward, he turns on her angrily. He explains that her reward was being able to remove her head from his mouth in safety.

## Intermediate English

A Wolf had been eating too greedily one day and got a bone stuck in his throat. He couldn't move it up or down, and with the bone there he also couldn't eat. In a panic, he went to see the Crane. His idea was that the Crane's long neck and bill could easily reach the bone.

Since the Crane was nervous about helping him, the Wolf promised her a fine reward if she did so. Eager for a reward, she agreed. As soon as the bone was out, the Wolf got up and went on his way. The Crane asked him for her reward, and he whirled on her angrily. Her reward, he explained, was being able to take her head back out of his mouth safely.

## Advanced English

A Wolf had been feasting too greedily one day and got a bone stuck crosswise in his throat. He couldn't move it either up or down, and with the bone where it was, he was unable to eat anything. In a panic, he rushed off to see the Crane, thinking that with her long neck and bill she would easily be able to reach the bone and pull it out. "I will reward you very handsomely," he told the Crane, "if you would just pull that bone out for me."

As you can imagine, the Crane was quite uneasy about the idea of putting her head in the Wolf's throat. But she was also desirous of receiving a reward, so she did what he asked her to do. When the Wolf felt that the bone was gone, he started to walk away. "But what about my reward!" the Crane called after him. "What?" snarled the Wolf, whirling around to face her. "Isn't it enough that I let you take your head from my mouth without snapping it off?"

## Moral

Expect no reward for serving the wicked.

## 10 Study Questions

(answers and explanations are below)

1) Feasting most nearly means
   a) eating a lot
   b) giving a dinner
   c) preparing food
   d) chewing loudly

2) Crosswise most nearly means
   a) difficultly
   b) uselessly
   c) diagonally

d) impossibly

3) Handsomely most nearly means
   a) readily
   b) handily
   c) perfectly
   d) substantially

4) Uneasy most nearly means
   a) angry
   b) troubled
   c) diseased
   d) unwelcome

5) Whirl around most nearly means
   a) spin in a circle
   b) flip upside down
   c) turn around quickly
   d) slide from side to side

6) How does the Wolf get the bone stuck in his throat?

7) Why does the Wolf ask the Crane to help him?

8) Why does the Crane agree to help?

9) What reward does the Wolf give to the Crane?

10) How does the story show the moral?

## Answers and Explanations

1) Feasting most nearly means EATING A LOT (a). To feast, as a verb, means

to eat a large meal or to eat extremely well.

2) Crosswise most nearly means DIAGONALLY (c). One meaning of crosswise is diagonally or "across" an area. Here, the bone is stuck with one end on one side of the Wolf's throat and the other end on the opposite side of his throat.

3) Handsomely most nearly means SUBSTANTIALLY (d). To reward someone "handsomely" means to reward them in a generous way, to reward them substantially.

4) Uneasy most nearly means TROUBLED (b). Someone who is uneasy is feeling anxiety or discomfort. We can say that someone who feels anxiety or discomfort is troubled (i.e., full of troubles or aware of their troubles).

5) Whirl around most nearly means SPIN AROUND IN A CIRCLE (a). Whirl around is a phrasal verb meaning to move in a circle or to turn around an axis like a wheel. In this story, "whirl around" suggests the Wolf turns around quickly to face the Crane. It emphasizes the danger the Crane faces.

6) The Wolf eats too much and too greedily, which leads to the bone getting stuck. "A Wolf had been feasting too greedily and got a bone stuck crosswise in his throat."

7) A Crane is a bird with a long, thin neck and a long, thin bill, so it is capable of reaching into the narrow throat of a Wolf and pulling something back out again.

8) The Crane agrees to help because she is eager for some kind of reward: "she was also desirous of receiving a reward, so she did what he asked her to do."

9) The Wolf gives no reward. The "reward" as he explains it is that he allows

37

her to live. "Isn't it enough that I let you take your head from my mouth without snapping it off?"

10) In the story, the Wolf represents wickedness or "the wicked" – meaning evil or wicked people. The Crane serves him expecting a reward, but the moral of the story informs us that we should expect no more of a reward than the Crane gets (being allowed to live) if we serve wicked people.

# 10

# The Tortoise and the Hare

### Basic English

In the woods one day a Rabbit makes fun of a Turtle for being so slow. The Turtle offers to run a race against the Rabbit to prove his ability to get around. The Rabbit agrees. He thinks a win is easy, and he can make fun of the Turtle afterward. They choose a path through the woods and begin the race.

The Rabbit races off until he is far ahead. He gets so far in front he decides to take a nap by the side of the road. The Turtle creeps along in his usual slow way. The Turtle eventually passes the sleeping Rabbit. When the Rabbit wakes up, the Turtle is almost at the finish line. The Rabbit tries desperately to catch him, but it is too late.

And that is how the Turtle won the race.

### Intermediate English

In the woods one day, a Hare was making fun of a Tortoise for being so slow. The Tortoise offered to run a race against the Hare to prove that, while he might be slow, he always got where he wanted to go. The Hare agreed to the race, thinking it would be easy to win and he could make fun of his friend afterward. They chose a long, winding path through the forest and began.

The Hare took off at once and quickly got very far ahead. In fact, he got so far ahead that he decided to take a nap by the side of the road until the

Tortoise caught up to him. Meanwhile, the Tortoise kept moving along in his usual slow manner. Eventually, he passed the sleeping Hare and moved steadily on to the finish line. The other animals in the forest cheered him on, waking the Hare. The Hare was shocked to see his friend so close to the finish and rushed to catch up. But he was too late.

That is how the Tortoise beat the Hare in a footrace.

## Advanced English

In the woods one day a Hare was mocking his old friend the Tortoise for being such a slow mover. "Do you ever get anywhere at all?" the Hare asked him, laughing. "I always get where I need to be," the Tortoise replied. "If you don't believe me, let's have a race, and I'll show you." The Hare agreed at once, thinking he'd win easily and mock his friend afterward. They picked out a long, winding path through the forest and began the race.

The Hare was off like a shot, running so fast that it wasn't long before he couldn't even see the Tortoise when he looked behind. As he neared the finish line, the Hare decided he'd have some fun with the Tortoise. "I'll nap here for a bit, wake up, then run rings around him on his way to the end." With that, he laid himself down to rest and was soon fast asleep. Meanwhile, the Tortoise kept trundling along in his usual slow, deliberate manner. Slowly, he passed by the sleeping Hare and soon neared the finish line. The other forest animals started laughing and cheering when they saw what was happening. The noise woke the Hare, who was much chagrined to see how far ahead the Tortoise had gotten. He ran as fast as he could to catch up, but the Tortoise was so far along it only took him a few short steps before he reached the end first.

And that was how the Tortoise beat the Hare in a footrace.

## Moral
The race is not always to the swift.

## 10 Study Questions
(answers and explanations are below)

1) Mocking most nearly means
   a) teasing
   b) detailing
   c) removing
   d) unsettling

2) Trundling most nearly means
   a) running lightly and easily
   b) spinning wildly and crazily
   c) moving slowly and heavily
   d) rolling purposefully and mildly

3) Chagrined most nearly means
   a) limited
   b) spirited
   c) humiliated
   d) determined

4) Deliberate most nearly means
   a) careful
   b) sprightly
   c) heedless
   d) unwarranted

5) Catch up most nearly means
   a) win
   b) reach
   c) defeat
   d) restrain

6) Why does the Tortoise offer to run a race?

7) Why does the Hare agree to run the race?

8) What does the Hare do that leads to him losing the race?

9) What wakes the Hare up?

10) How does the story show the moral?

## Answers and Explanations

1) Mocking most nearly means TEASING (a). To mock someone is to tease them, often in a hurtful or embarrassing manner.

2) Trundling most nearly means MOVING SLOWLY AND HEAVILY (c). To trundle is to move in a very slow, heavy way. Sometimes this word is used as part of the verbal phrase "trundle along," which has a similar meaning.

3) Chagrined most nearly means HUMILIATED (c). Chagrin is a feeling of embarrassment or humiliation, usually as a result of one's own failing. In the story, the Hare is chagrined because his own folly led to his losing a race he should have won easily.

4) Deliberate most nearly means CAREFUL (a). Deliberate as an adjective means careful, considered, planned. Something which is deliberate has been thought about.

5) Catch up most nearly means REACH (b). Catch up is a verbal phrase with several meanings, one of which is to reach someone who is ahead.

6) The Tortoise offers to run the race to show the Hare that even though he may be slow he always gets to his destination. "I always get where I need to be... let's have a race and I'll show you."

7) The Hare agrees to run the race because he thinks it will offer him another opportunity to mock the Tortoise. "The Hare agreed at once, thinking he'd

win easily and mock his friend afterward."

8) The Hare decides to take a nap by the side of the road. It's another way for him to embarrass the Tortoise if he can sleep for a while, wake up, then win the race anyway. "As he neared the finish line, the Hare decided he'd have some fun with the Tortoise. 'I'll nap here for a bit, wake up, then run rings around him on his way to the end.'"

9) The laughter and cheers of the other forest animals is what wakes the Hare. "The other forest animals started laughing and cheering when they saw what was happening. The noise woke the Hare."

10) The moral means that it isn't always the fastest runner who wins a race—that is, physical skills are not the only factor in deciding results. The Hare is obviously faster than the Tortoise, but his overconfidence in his skill leads to him making a mistake (deciding to take a nap) which he should not make.

# 11

# The Goose that Laid Golden Eggs

### Basic English

A farmer has a wonderful Goose. Each morning this Goose lays a single glittering, golden egg. The farmer takes these eggs to market and soon begins to become rich. He also becomes impatient with the Goose because she only lays one egg each day. His riches are not growing fast enough.

So, one day when he finishes counting his money, he thinks of a way to get all the eggs at once. He grabs a knife, kills the Goose, and cuts it open. But he does not find a single golden egg inside. And now the wonderful Goose is dead.

### Intermediate English

There was a farmer who had the most wonderful Goose. Each morning when he came to her nest, she laid a beautiful, glittering, golden egg. He took these eggs to market and soon began to become rich. But he also became impatient. At the rate of one egg a day, his riches were not growing fast enough.

So, one day after he had finished counting his money, he thought of a way to get all the eggs at once. He would kill the Goose and cut it open. He grabbed a cleaver and killed the Goose, but he didn't find a single golden egg inside of her. And now his wonderful Goose was dead.

## Advanced English

There once was a farmer who possessed the most wonderful Goose one could imagine because each morning when he visited her nest, he found she had laid a beautiful, glittering, golden egg. He sold these eggs at the market each day, and soon found himself becoming rich. But along with his riches came impatience. "Why must she provide only one egg each day," he asked himself. Easy as the work was for him, his riches simply weren't growing fast enough to suit him.

So, one day after he had finished counting his money, the idea occurred to him that he could obtain all the eggs at once by killing the Goose and cutting it open. He laid hold of a cleaver and lopped off the Goose's head, but as soon as the deed was done, he found not a single golden egg inside. And now his precious Goose was dead.

## Moral
In striving for more one can lose everything.

## 10 Study Questions
(answers and explanations are below)

1) Possess most nearly means
   a) own
   b) make
   c) utilize
   d) capture

2) Glittering most nearly means
   a) seeing
   b) shining
   c) spraying
   d) straining

3) Impatience most nearly means

a) deep sadness

b) sudden despair

c) sharp melancholy

d) restless eagerness

4) Obtain most nearly means

a) get

b) spot

c) claim

d) defend

5) Lop off most nearly means

a) dip out

b) spin off

c) cut away

d) smash in

6) What does the farmer's wonderful Goose provide him?

7) Why is the farmer impatient with the Goose?

8) What does he decide to do to improve his situation?

9) What is the result of his action?

10) How does the story show the moral?

## Answers and Explanations

1) Possess most nearly means OWN (a). To possess something is to own or have it.

2) Glittering most nearly means SHINING (b). Glittering means to shine

with a shimmering or sparkling light the way gems or gold can shine in the light.

3) Impatience most nearly means RESTLESS EAGERNESS (d). Patience is the ability to accept delay, trouble, or suffering without getting angry or upset. Impatience is the opposite—an inability to do this. Impatience can also be defined as a restless eagerness for something (usually due to being unable to accept any delays).

4) Obtain most nearly means GET (a). Obtain is a more high-level vocabulary word for describing getting, acquiring, or securing something.

5) Lop off most nearly means CUT AWAY (c). Lop off is a verbal phrase meaning to cut something off or away, especially when this is done quickly and without much care or concern. In the story, the farmer decides to "lop off" the head of his wonderful Goose thinking it will benefit him, but he is wrong.

6) The farmer's wonderful Goose provides him with a single "beautiful, glittering, golden egg" each morning.

7) The farmer becomes impatient with the Goose because he begins to feel that one golden egg a day is not enough. He wants to get richer, faster: "his riches simply weren't growing fast enough to suit him."

8) The farmer decides to get "all the eggs at once" by opening the Goose up. His idea is that the eggs must all be inside the Goose somewhere, but she only releases one each day. Of course, this would be silly as one small goose couldn't hold more than a few eggs inside its body.

9) The result of the Farmer's action is that the Goose is killed but he has no more golden eggs. There were none inside of the Goose and now the animal which produced the wonderful eggs is dead and will produce no more.

10) The farmer was "striving for more" by trying to get a lot of eggs all at once instead of accepting one golden egg each day. He lost everything because by killing the Goose he ensured that he would get no more golden eggs at all. "Killing the goose that laid golden eggs" is a kind of saying in English which means to foolishly destroy or ruin a source of benefit to oneself.

# 12

# The Fox and the Goat

### Basic English

A Fox falls into a well one day and is not able to get out. After a long time, a Goat comes by the well. The goat is thirsty. He thinks the Fox is in the well to drink the water. He asks the Fox if the water is any good. The Fox says that it is, so the Goat jumps in and drinks. The Fox jumps on the Goat's back, and from there jumps out of the well.

The Goat now realizes he is stuck, and he begs the Fox to help him. But the Fox is already on his way into the woods. He tells the Goat he needs to be more careful. Check the situation before you jump in.

### Intermediate English

A Fox fell into a well one day and couldn't get back out again. After a long time, a thirsty Goat came by looking for something to drink. The Goat asked the Fox if the water in the well was any good. The crafty Fox replied that the water was delicious, so the Goat jumped in and started drinking. As he did so, the Fox jumped onto his back and then scrambled up out of the well.

The Goat quickly realized he was stuck and begged the Fox to come help him out. But the Fox was already well on his way into the woods. As he ran, he called out over his shoulder that the Goat should be more cautious before jumping into situations he doesn't understand.

## Advanced English

One day a clumsy Fox fell into a well and couldn't get himself back out again. He lay there for a long time before a thirsty Goat happened by, looking for something to drink. "How's the water?" the Goat asked. "Delicious," the crafty Fox assured him, "Why don't you join me?" The Goat jumped in and started happily drinking up the water. As he did so, the Fox leapt onto his back and from there managed to scramble up out of the well.

Now realizing his plight, the Goat cried out: "Come help me, Mr. Fox!" But the Fox was already well on his way to the safety of the woods. "If you had any more sense, my friend," he called out over his shoulder, "you would've checked more carefully before you dove in."

## Moral
Look before you leap.

## 10 Study Questions
(answers and explanations are below)

1) Clumsy most nearly means
   a) simple
   b) gawky
   c) foolish
   d) supine

2) Assure most nearly means
   a) disturb
   b) confirm
   c) assuage
   d) persuade

3) Scramble most nearly means
   a) climb
   b) spring

THE FOX AND THE GOAT

c) pretend

d) absolve

4) Plight most nearly means
   a) event
   b) solace
   c) education
   d) predicament

5) Dive in most nearly means
   a) leap into
   b) turn from
   c) run away
   d) look about

6) How did the Fox end up in the well?

7) How does the Fox trick the Goat into jumping into the well?

8) How does the Fox use the Goat to escape?

9) How does the Fox respond to the Goat's request for help?

10) How does the story show the moral?

## Answers and Explanations

1) Clumsy most nearly means GAWKY (b). To be clumsy means to move in an awkward or graceless way—to be prone to accidents or mistakes. Gawky is another word used to describe this. In the story, the Fox is clumsy because his movements led him to fall into a well, which was clearly a bad accident.

2) Assure most nearly means CONFIRM (b). To assure someone means to tell

them something positively or confidently so as to dispel any doubts. Confirm means to establish that something is true or correct, so this word is the closest match.

3) Scramble most nearly means CLIMB (a). One of the meanings of scramble is to move or climb quickly but with difficulty, usually by using your hands to assist. Scramble often appears in the phrasal verb 'scramble up', as it does in this story. In the story, the Fox scrambles up out of the well, meaning that he uses all four of his legs to pull himself out with some difficulty.

4) Plight most nearly means PREDICAMENT (d). To be "in a plight" means to be in a difficult or dangerous situation. A predicament is a difficult, unpleasant, or embarrassing situation, so this word is the best match.

5) Dive in most nearly means LEAP INTO (a). Dive in is a phrasal verb meaning to literally leap or jump into something such as a pool. A well with water is somewhat similar to a pool, so the expression works in this story. But the phrasal verb also means to get into a situation without thinking about it—which is what the poor Goat in the story does. So, at the end the Fox is telling the Goat that he "dove in" to the well and that he "dove in" to a dangerous situation without thinking ahead.

6) The Fox fell in due to his own clumsiness.

7) The Fox tricks the Goat by telling him the water is "delicious" and asking the Goat to join him. The Fox says nothing about being stuck down in the well, so the Goat doesn't realize that the Fox is in a dangerous situation. We also know the Goat is thirsty, so perhaps he is vulnerable to being tricked about the water in the well.

8) The Fox uses the Goat by jumping onto his back and from that height he is just able to get himself out of the well: "the Fox leapt onto his back and from there managed to scramble up out of the well."

9) The Fox responds by calling out over his shoulder than the Goat should have been more careful before jumping in.

10) The moral is similar in meaning to what the Fox tells the Goat as he is running off to safety. The idea is that before one gets involved in a situation—before one jumps in or leaps in to do something—one should be more aware of what the situation is. Take a good look first. The Goat should have looked more carefully before he jumped into the well, and if he had he wouldn't have been stuck there.

# 13

# The Lion and the Mouse

### Basic English

A Lion sleeps in the forest one day. He rests his head on his paws. A little Mouse runs up. She does not expect to see a Lion there and runs into his nose. The Lion wakes up. He is angry. He puts a paw on the tail of the Mouse and prepares to smash her. She begs him to spare her life. She says she will repay him one day if he does. The Lion laughs at this. He is generous of heart, so he lets her go.

A few days later, the Lion chases his prey through the forest. He gets caught in a hunter's trap. Unable to free himself, he roars with anger. His roars fill the forest. The Mouse hears him and comes to see. She chews at the ropes which hold the Lion in place. In a short time, he is free again. She tells him that sometimes even a Mouse can help a Lion.

### Intermediate English

A lion was sleeping in the forest one day, with his head resting on his paws, when a timid little Mouse came running up. Not expecting to see a Lion there, she ran right into his nose, waking him up. Angry at being awakened, the Lion put one of his paws on the Mouse's tail and prepared to smash her. She begged him to spare her life, saying that she would repay him one day if he did. The Lion was amused by her offer and laughed at her. But he was also generous of heart, so he let her go.

A few days later, the Lion was stalking his prey in the forest when he got caught in a hunter's trap. Unable to free himself, he roared with anger. His voice filled the forest until the Mouse heard him and came running. Seeing the situation, she chewed at the ropes which held the Lion in place until they broke. When the Lion was free, the Mouse told him that he now saw that even a Mouse could help a Lion.

## Advanced English

A Lion was asleep in the forest one day, with his head resting gently on his paws. A timid little Mouse came running up, and, not expecting to see the Lion there, she ran right into his nose, waking him up. Angry at being roused in this manner, the Lion lay one of his paws on the poor Mouse's tail and prepared to smash her. "Please spare me," the poor Mouse begged, "and one day I will surely repay you." The Lion was much amused to think that a little Mouse could ever help him, and he chuckled mightily at her offer. But he was also generous of heart, so he let the harmless creature go.

A few days later, while stalking his prey in the forest, the Lion was suddenly caught in the strong ropes of a hunter's trap. Unable to free himself, he roared with anger until his voice filled the surrounding forest. Eventually, the Mouse heard him and came running. She gnawed with her sharp teeth at the ropes which held the Lion in place, and in a short time he was free again. "You laughed when I said I would repay you," she told him, "but now you see that sometimes even a Mouse can help a Lion."

## Moral
A kindness is never wasted.

## 10 Study Questions
(answers and explanations are below)

1) Timid most nearly means
   a) slight

b) meek

c) pretty

d) careful

2) Roused most nearly means

  a) handled

  b) bothered

  c) promoted

  d) awakened

3) Repay most nearly means

  a) value

  b) prepare

  c) determine

  d) compensate

4) Stalking most nearly means

  a) watching idly

  b) pursuing quietly

  c) conversing readily

  b) investigating eagerly

5) Gnaw most nearly means

  a) split

  b) rend

  c) chew

  d) align

6) How does the Mouse wake up the Lion?

7) Why does the Lion let the Mouse go?

8) What happens to the Lion that requires the Mouse's aid?

9) How does the Mouse help the Lion?

10) How does the story show the moral?

## Answers and Explanations

1) Timid most nearly means MEEK (b). To be timid is to have a lack of courage or confidence, to be easily frightened. Meek is a synonym for someone who is easily frightened or without confidence.

2) Roused most nearly means AWAKENED (d). One of the main meanings of rouse is to bring out of sleep, so 'awakened' is a close synonym.

3) Repay most nearly means COMPENSATE (d). To repay is to return a debt or pay back something which was owed. Compensate is another way of saying to pay back or return the value of something.

4) Stalking most nearly means PURSUING QUIETLY (b). Animals stalk their prey by quietly and carefully pursuing them until pouncing on them. Lions are a notable animal that stalks its meals.

5) Gnaw most nearly means CHEW (c). To gnaw on something is to chew on it, usually with the idea that one is persistent in the chewing. In the story, the idea is that the Mouse must spend some time focused on chewing at the thick ropes which hold the Lion.

6) The Mouse wakes the Lion by running into him: "she ran right into his nose, waking him up."

7) The Lion is amused by the Mouse's promise to repay him for letting her go, but we also are told that he is "generous of heart" so he lets her go. Mice are not a usual food source for lions because they are too small anyway.

8) The Lion gets "caught in the strong ropes of a hunter's trap" and is not able to get himself out of it. Lions' teeth are not well built for chewing ropes, but the teeth of mice certainly are.

9) The Mouse helps the Lion by chewing at the ropes of the trap until they break, and the Lion can get free. "She gnawed with her sharp teeth at the ropes which held the Lion in place, and in a short time he was free again."

10) In the story, the kindness is the Lion letting the Mouse go because she was harmless to him and only awakened him by a foolish mistake. This kindness was not wasted because the Mouse repaid him by saving his life. Had he remained in the hunter's trap he would eventually have been found and killed by the hunters. The idea in the story is that sometimes a kindness will be repaid in some unexpected way—even by someone who we might not even think could help us out in the future.

# 14

# The Crow and the Pitcher

### Basic English

The weather is hot one summer, and none of the animals can find much to drink. A thirsty Crow finds a pitcher of water. But the pitcher is high with a narrow neck. The Crow is unable to reach the water at the bottom of it. He is uncertain what to do. Then he gets an idea. He picks up some small rocks and drops them into the pitcher. The water level in the pitcher rises slowly until it reaches the top. The Crow is now able to reach the water and drink.

### Intermediate English

One summer when the weather was hot, none of the animals could find much to drink. A thirsty Crow came across a pitcher of water. But the pitcher was high with a narrow neck, so the Crow couldn't reach the water at the bottom of it. He didn't know what to do at first, but presently an idea came to him. He picked up some small rocks and dropped them into the pitcher. The water level in the pitcher rose little by little until reaching the very top, where the Crow could drink it.

### Advanced English

During a spell of hot weather one summer, when none of the animals could find much to drink, a thirsty Crow came across a pitcher of water. But the pitcher was high with a narrow neck, and no matter how hard the Crow tried he couldn't reach the water at the bottom. He was about to despair when an idea came to him. He picked up some little pebbles and dropped them one by one into the pitcher. Slowly, the water level in the pitcher rose and rose until at last it had reached the very top of the pitcher where the Crow could reach it.

## Moral
Use your good wits to help yourself in a pinch.

## 10 Study Questions
(answers and explanations are below)

1) Spell most nearly means
   a) limited area
   b) intense heat
   c) period of time
   d) unspecified day

2) Pitcher most nearly means
   a) jug
   b) ladle
   c) bottle
   d) canvas

3) Despair most nearly means
   a) weep
   b) leave
   c) give up
   d) move out

4) Pebble most nearly means
   a) dirt

   b) gem
   c) stone
   d) handle

5) Narrow most nearly means
   a) thin
   b) open
   c) broad
   d) planed

6) Why is the Crow so thirsty?

7) Why does the Crow want to give up?

8) Why doesn't the Crow give up?

9) What does he do to reach the water?

10) How does the story show the moral?

## Answers and Explanations

1) Spell most nearly means PERIOD OF TIME (c). One of the meanings of spell is "a period of time," especially a period of some particular kind of weather such as heat or cold. A "spell of hot weather" like in the story is a very common use of this word.

2) Pitcher most nearly means JUG (a). A pitcher is a large container for holding and pouring liquids. A jug is a similar kind of container.

3) Despair most nearly means GIVE UP (c). To despair is to lose hope or to be without hope, so feelings of despair often precede a decision to give up or to stop trying.

4) Pebble most nearly means STONE (c). A pebble is a small rock or stone.

5) Narrow most nearly means THIN (a). A narrow neck on the pitcher means that it is too thin at the top for the Crow to fit his head in and reach the water stored at the bottom.

6) The Crow is thirsty because the weather is hot over time (a "spell of hot weather") and none of the animals can find much to drink.

7) The Crow is about to despair because "no matter how hard the Crow tried he couldn't reach the water" in the pitcher.

8) The Crow doesn't give up because he gets an idea of how to reach the water another way. Instead of trying to reach the water he will do something that will make the water level rise until he can reach it.

9) The Crow picks up pebbles and drops them into the pitcher. The pebbles fall to the bottom and slowly push the water upward as they fill in the bottom. Eventually the water level rises to the top of the pitcher where the Crow can drink easily.

10) The Crow is "in a pinch" (a difficult situation) because he needs water but is unable to reach it by any normal means. He uses his "good wits" to look at his situation in a different way. The way he uses the pebbles is a clever idea that allows him to reach his goal in a different way—by having the water rise to meet him.

# 15

# The Tortoise and the Ducks

### Basic English

One day a Turtle looks up and sees the birds above him. They seem to fly so happily in the air. He feels discontent with his life on the ground. A pair of Ducks lands nearby, and he tells them his troubles. They offer to show him the world of the sky. They explain that if he holds a stick with his teeth, they can carry him into the air where he can see everything. But they warn him not to speak during the trip.

The Turtle agrees and grabs hold of the stick. The Ducks each take hold of one end of the stick and the three fly off. As they fly around, a Crow comes by. He is surprised by the sight of a flying Turtle. He calls out to the King of the Turtles. The Turtle opens his mouth to reply, but as he does so he loses his hold of the stick and falls to the ground where he is dashed to pieces.

### Intermediate English

One day a Tortoise looked up and saw how happily the birds flew in the air above him. He felt discontented with his life on the ground. A pair of Ducks landed nearby, so he told them his troubles. The Ducks offered to show him the world of the sky. They explained that if he would just hold a stick with his teeth they could carry him up into the air where he could see everything. But they also warned him not to speak during the trip or he would be sorry.

The Tortoise agreed at once and seized a stick firmly in his teeth. The Ducks each took hold of one end of the stick and the three took off into the air. As they were flying, a Crow flew by. Surprised by the sight, he cried out to the King of the Tortoises. The Tortoise opened his mouth to reply, but as he did so he lost hold of the stick and fell to the ground where he was dashed to pieces.

## Advanced English

One day a Tortoise looked up and saw how happily the birds flew above him in the blue sky. "They get to see the whole world," he said to himself discontentedly, "while I am stuck here on the ground." When a pair of Ducks happened to land nearby, he told them his troubles. "We can help you see the world," the pair explained. "Take hold of this stick with your teeth and we will carry you far up in the air where you can see the whole countryside. But be sure to keep quiet during the trip, or you'll be sorry."

The Tortoise gladly agreed to the plan and seized a stick firmly in his teeth as he was instructed. The Ducks took hold of the stick at each end and away they went. As they flew through the air a Crow happened by. He was startled by the sight of a Tortoise flying through the air with such an escort. "This must be the King of the Tortoises," he cried out to them. "I certainly am," the Tortoise began, but as soon as he opened his mouth to speak these foolish words, he lost hold of the stick. Down he fell to the ground, where he was dashed to pieces.

## Moral
Vanity can lead to misfortune.

## 10 Study Questions
(answers and explanations are below)

1) Discontented most nearly means
   a) impure
   a) uncertain

b) unplanned

d) dissatisfied

2) Happen to most nearly means
   a) come into mind
   b) occur by chance
   c) take place suddenly
   b) work according to plan

3) Take hold most nearly means
   a) grab onto
   b) put to use
   c) tear apart
   d) drop in parts

4) Startle most nearly means
   a) prepare
   b) magnify
   c) surprise
   d) intensify

5) Dash to pieces most nearly means
   a) fall suddenly
   b) send on a journey
   c) carry away at once
   d) break into fragments

6) Why is the Tortoise feeling discontented?

7) What do the Ducks offer the Tortoise?

8) What warning do the Ducks give the Tortoise?

9) How do the Ducks carry the Tortoise into the air?

10) How does the story show the moral?

## Answers and Explanations

1) Discontented most nearly means DISSATISFIED (d). To be discontented means to be not satisfied with one's circumstances. The Tortoise in the story is not satisfied with his life on the ground and wants to experience something like what the birds experience.

2) Happen to most nearly means OCCUR BY CHANCE (b). The verbal phrase "happen to [verb]" means for something to be done or to occur by chance. In the story, the Ducks just "happened to land" nearby as the Tortoise was thinking about bird life. It was a chance event, not something planned or decided.

3) Take hold most nearly means GRAB ONTO (a). To "take hold" of something means to grab or grasp it firmly. Usually, it means to grab it with your hands, but in the story the Tortoise "takes hold" of the stick with his mouth since he has no hands to hold the stick the way a human could.

4) Startle most nearly means SURPRISE (c). To startle means to cause a person or animal to feel a sudden shock or alarm. In the story, the Crow is shocked or startled by the sight of a Tortoise flying up in the air with two Ducks carrying him.

5) Dash to pieces most nearly means BREAK INTO FRAGMENTS (d). Dash to pieces is an English idiom meaning for something to break into small pieces or fragments. In the story, it means that the unfortunate Tortoise was killed.

6) The Tortoise feels discontented because he sees the birds flying happily

above him. The birds seem to have an experience he is unable to have: "They get to see the whole world... while I am stuck here on the ground."

7) The Ducks offer to help the Tortoise see the world by taking him on a trip through the air.

8) They warn the Tortoise to "keep quiet during the trip, or you'll be sorry." Meaning not to speak or he will regret it. Since the trip is only made possible by the Tortoise holding a stick with his mouth, he will be unable to use his mouth to speak.

9) The Tortoise grabs the middle of a stick with his mouth, then the two Ducks grab either end of the stick in their mouths and they lift the Tortoise into the air with them.

10) In the story, a Crow remarks that "This must be the King of the Tortoises" when he sees the Tortoise flying by. It is vanity for the Tortoise to respond to this, which he does by saying "I certain am." This vanity leads directly to misfortune because by speaking he loses his grip on the stick and falls to his death.

# 16

# The Town Mouse and the Country Mouse

A Town Mouse goes to visit her relative the Country Mouse. The Country Mouse serves her cousin a simple meal. The Town Mouse eats politely but without pleasure. After the meal, the two have a long talk. The Town Mouse describes the wonders of city life. That night, the Country Mouse dreams about all the luxuries of the city. The next day, when the Town Mouse asks her cousin to visit her home in the city, she agrees.

The Town Mouse lives in a mansion in the city. When they arrive, the dining room is full of food. As the Country Mouse prepares to nibble on some food, they hear a cat scratch at the door. The two mice hide from the cat. For a long time, they hardly dare to breathe. After a time, they emerge from hiding. As they do so, the back door opens, and the house servants come in to clean up the room. A dog comes in with them and sniffs around for the mice.

The Country Mouse rushes back to the hiding hole and grabs her bag. As she leaves for home, she tells her cousin that she prefers the peace and security of the countryside.

## Intermediate English

A Town Mouse went to visit her cousin the Country Mouse. The Country

Mouse served a simple meal, which the Town Mouse ate politely but without much enjoyment. After the meal, the two cousins talked for a long time. The Town Mouse described all the wonders of her life in the city. That night, as they slept in the Country Mouse's simple home, the Country Mouse dreamed of the luxuries of the city. The next day, when the Town Mouse asked her to come visit her home in the city, she quickly agreed.

The Town Mouse lived in a mansion in the city. When the two got there, they found the dining room full of the leavings of a most excellent banquet. But just as the Country Mouse was about to nibble on some of the food, the sound of a cat scratching at the door scared them off. For a long time, the two mice lay hidden in fear. Just as they felt ready to emerge again, the back door opened, and the house servants came in to clean up the room. A great dog came in with them, who started sniffing around for the mice.

The Country Mouse had enough. She grabbed her bag and umbrella and headed for the exit. On her way out, she told her cousin that she preferred the peace and security of the countryside to the pleasures of the city.

## Advanced English

A Town Mouse once visited her relative who lived in the country. The Country Mouse served her a simple meal of roots and acorns with nothing more than a splash of cold water to drink. The Town Mouse ate but sparingly, nibbling a little of this and a little of that and making it clear that she was eating merely to be polite. After the meal, the cousins had a long talk—or rather, the Town Mouse talked about her wonderful life in the city while the Country Mouse listened. As they slept that night in the Country Mouse's unadorned nest in a hedgerow, the Country Mouse dreamed about all the luxuries and wonders of city life that her cousin had described for her. The next day, when the Town Mouse asked the Country Mouse to visit her home in the city, the latter readily agreed.

They reached the mansion in town where the Town Mouse lived, and in the dining room they were delighted to find the leavings of a marvelous banquet. The table was spread with sweetmeats and jellies, pastries of all kinds, delicious cheeses, and in all the most tempting food a mouse could wish for. But just as the Country Mouse was about to nibble on a bit of pastry, they heard a cat scratching and mewing at the door. In great fear for their lives, the two mice scurried off to a hiding place. They lay there for a long time, as still as death, scarcely daring to breathe. Finally, they recovered enough of their courage to poke a nose out of their hiding place—but as they did so the back door suddenly swung open and in came the house servants to clean up the room. And with them came a great romping dog, who sniffed about the room searching for the mice.

The Country Mouse grabbed up her bag and umbrella and headed for the exit. "You may have luxuries and dainties that I lack," she told her cousin as she hurried away, "but I prefer the peace and security of the countryside!"

<u>Moral</u>
Poverty with security is better than plenty in the midst of fear and uncertainty.

<u>10 Study Questions</u>
(answers and explanations are below)

1) Sparingly most nearly means
   a) in a bad mood
   b) without concern
   c) in small quantities
   d) with obvious distaste

2) Nibble most nearly means
   a) paw at
   b) chew a lot
   c) lick one's lips
   d) take small bites

3) Latter most nearly means
   a) cousin

a) one close by

c) second of two

d) person of interest

4) Banquet most nearly means
 a) meal
 b) room
 c) detail
 d) dessert

5) Scurry off most nearly means
 a) run away
 b) circle over
 c) duck under
 d) play around

6) How does the Town Mouse eat the simple food of the Country Mouse?

7) Why does the Country Mouse agree to visit the city?

8) What is the first thing that scares the two mice into hiding?

9) Does the Country Mouse enjoy the luxuries of the city?

10) How does the story show the moral?

## Answers and Explanations

1) Sparingly most nearly means IN SMALL QUANTITIES (c). When something is done sparingly it is done as little as possible or with as little effort as possible.

2) Nibble most nearly means TAKE SMALL BITES (d). To nibble at something

is to take small bites out of it, and a nibble (as a noun) is a small bite.

3) Latter most nearly means SECOND OF TWO (c). English uses the words 'former' and 'latter' to mean the first of two and the second of two, respectively. In the story, the sentence is: "when the Town Mouse asked the Country Mouse to visit her home in the city, the latter readily agreed." The "latter" in this sentence is the Country Mouse because she was the second of the two persons mentioned. This is a common use of this word. In that sentence, the Town Mouse would be the "former."

4) Banquet most nearly means MEAL (a). A banquet is a special or sumptuous meal, usually with lots of different foods served for a large group of people.

5) Scurry off most nearly means RUN AWAY (a). Scurry off is a verbal phrase meaning to move fast with small, quick steps.

6) The Town Mouse eats only a little bit of the simple food and does so only out of politeness. She eats "sparingly" by "nibbling a little of this and a little of that" and "making it clear that she was eating merely to be polite."

7) The Country Mouse agrees to visit the city because the Town Mouse describes "her wonderful life in the city" and the Country Mouse dreams about "all the luxuries and wonders of city life that her cousin had described for her." She wants to see the wonderful things her cousin was talking about. The simple country life isn't very exciting to her.

8) The first thing that scares the two mice into hiding is the sound of a cat: "they heard a cat scratching and mewing at the door."

9) The Country Mouse never enjoys the luxuries of the city. Before she can eat anything, the cat scares them away. Then people arrive to clean up the food. Then a dog comes in and starts sniffing around trying to find the mice. She decides to return home instead.

10) The Country Mouse does not have very much in the way of exciting food or luxuries. Compared to the luxuries of the city, she lives in poverty. But she also doesn't have much to worry about, she has a certain amount of security. The Town Mouse has great plenty living in the city, but the great plenty also comes with issues like cats, dogs, and people intruding all the time. At the end, the Country Mouse decides that her poverty with security is better than the Town Mouse's plenty surrounded by fear and uncertainty.

# 17

# The Leap at Paris

Basic English

There is a man who likes to travel. He goes to many foreign countries. When he returns home, he tells everyone about his adventures. He brags about many great actions. One action he brags about is a long jump. He claims he can jump further than anyone. He made a world record jump in Paris. Everyone in Paris can confirm it and prove this is true. The people in his town do not believe him. One of them tells him to prove it by repeating the jump. This man tells the traveler to pretend their hometown is Paris and repeat his record jump.

Intermediate English

There was a man who loved to travel to foreign countries. When he returned home, he always told everyone about his wonderful adventures. He bragged about all the great actions he had performed. One such action was an impressive long jump. He claimed that when he was in Paris, he performed a world record jump longer than anyone else had ever managed. One of his countrymen then asked him to prove his claim by repeating the act where everyone could see. Just pretend that their hometown is Paris and repeat that record jump.

## Advanced English

A certain man who loved to visit foreign lands could talk of nothing else when he returned home save the marvelous adventures he had met with and the great deeds he had performed while abroad. This man would go on at such length that he often tired out his listeners with his boasting. Well, it so happened that one of the great deeds he talked about was a great leap he had made while in Paris. "It was a world record," he assured his listeners. "Anyone in Paris could confirm that I did it." "No need of witnesses," one of his hearers said. "Just pretend that here is Paris and show us how far you can jump."

## Moral

Deeds count for more than boasting words.

## 10 Study Questions

(answers and explanations are below)

1) Marvelous most nearly means
   a) manifold
   b) pretentious
   c) cumbersome
   d) extraordinary

2) Boasting most nearly means
   a) babbling
   b) bragging
   c) speaking
   d) speechifying

3) At length most nearly means
   a) in great detail
   b) until late at night
   c) repeating oneself
   d) without any questions

4) Deed most nearly means
   a) simple lie
   b) certain work
   c) old deception
   d) impressive act

5) Confirm most nearly means
   a) assure
   b) prepare
   c) determine
   d) overwhelm

6) What does the traveler like to do when he returns home?

7) What does the traveler do to annoy his listeners?

8) What does the traveler brag about?

9) What do the people in his town suggest that he do to prove himself?

10) How does the story show the moral?

## Answers and Explanations

1) Marvelous most nearly means EXTRAORDINARY (d). Something which is marvelous is causing great wonder or extraordinary in some way.

2) Boasting means BRAGGING (b). To boast is another way of saying to brag, which means to talk with excessive pride about oneself or one's achievements.

3) At length means IN GREAT DETAIL (a). To go on at great length means to speak for a long time and in great detail about something. Option B "until late at night" is not necessarily meant by "at length," although in some contexts

someone who went on "at length" might indeed go on until late at night. But it would always mean that they were speaking in great detail about something, so option A is the best choice.

4) Deed most nearly means IMPRESSIVE ACT (d). A deed can be an act of any kind, but often the word is used to mean some kind of impressive or marvelous act which is worthy of notice or worthy of being told.

5) Confirm most nearly means ASSURE (a). To confirm something is to establish the truth or correctness of it, which is another way of saying to assure someone about it.

6) The traveler likes to talk about all the things he did on his trips: "the marvelous adventures he had met with and the great deeds he had performed while abroad."

7) The traveler annoys his listeners by talking too long and too boastingly about himself: "This man would go on at such length that he often tired out his listeners with his boasting."

8) The traveler brags about making a "world record" jump while he was in Paris: "one of the great deeds he told about was a great leap he had made while in Paris."

9) One of the listeners suggests that the man repeat his jump to demonstrate his ability to do it. After all, the ability to jump a long way has nothing to do with whether one is in Paris or in one's own hometown. "Just pretend that here is Paris and show us how far you can jump."

10) The moral is that an actual act demonstrated to people is of more value than just the words saying you can do something. The traveler has many words to describe his deeds, but we never see him actually perform anything he talks about. One suspects that he may have never done any of these deeds

since there is no one around to confirm whether he did them or not.

# 18

# Belling the Cat

### Basic English

The Mice call a meeting one day to decide how to deal with their enemy, the Cat. They want to find a way of warning themselves about the Cat so they can hide from her. As it is, they live in fear of her every day. Many plans come up, but none seems good enough. Then a young Mouse gets up with a suggestion. He says they can hang a bell around the Cat's neck. When the bell rings, they have their warning.

The Mice like this plan a lot. They cheer the young Mouse. But as they do so an old Mouse gets up. He asks one simple question: Who will bell the Cat?

### Intermediate English

The Mice called a meeting one day to decide how best to deal with their old enemy, the Cat. They wanted to find a way of warning themselves about her approach. They needed time to run and hide. They were living in fear of her every day. Many plans were brought up, but none of them seemed good enough. Then a young Mouse got up and offered his suggestion. If they hung a bell around the Cat's neck, whenever the bell rung, they would know the Cat was coming.

The Mice were pleased by this plan and started cheering the young Mouse. But as they were cheering an old Mouse got up and asked them one simple question: Who will bell the Cat?

## Advanced English

One day the Mice held a meeting to decide how best to deal with their old enemy, the Cat. They wanted to find at least some kind of early warning system that would tell them when the cat was approaching so they would have time to run and hide. Something had to be done, because the Mice were living in daily fear of the Cat's claws and hardly dared stir from their homes. Many plans were discussed but none were thought good enough until at last a young Mouse arose and said: "I have a plan that seems very simple, but I know it'll work. All we have to do is hang a bell about the Cat's neck. When we hear the bell ringing, we'll know immediately that she's coming."

All the Mice were pleasantly surprised by the young Mouse's plan. No one could believe that such a marvelous idea had not come up before. But in the midst of the rejoicing over their good fortune a wise old Mouse arose and said: "I confess that the plan of my young friend, here, is quite good. Yet I'm curious about one thing: Who will bell the Cat?"

## Moral

It is one thing to say something should be done and another to do it.

## 10 Study Questions

(answers and explanations are below)

1) Approach most nearly means
   a) tear apart
   b) break into
   c) come near
   d) wander off

2) Stir from most nearly means
   a) enter into
   b) alter thinking

c) move upward

d) change position

3) Midst most nearly means

a) on top of

b) by the side of

c) in the middle of

d) on the edges of

4) Rejoicing most nearly means

a) hungering

b) wandering

c) celebrating

d) deliberating

5) Arise most nearly means

a) dip in

b) lift off

c) come by

d) stand up

6) What are the mice looking for at the beginning of the story?

7) Why is the Cat such a problem for the mice?

8) How do the mice respond to the young mouse's suggestion?

9) What problem does the old mouse raise?

10) How does the story show the moral?

## Answers and Explanations

1) Approach most nearly means COME NEAR (c). To approach something is to come near it. In the story, the mice want some way of knowing when the Cat is approaching them—that is, they want to know when danger is near.

2) Stir from most nearly means CHANGE POSITION (d). Stir from is a verbal phrase meaning to change position or leave a place. In the story, the mice are afraid to leave their homes because the Cat could come upon them at any moment.

3) Midst most nearly means IN THE MIDDLE OF (c). In the story, the mice are all celebrating and in the middle of that the old mouse stands up to ask his simple question.

4) Rejoicing most nearly means CELEBRATING (c). Rejoicing is great joy, jubilation, which are emotions related to celebration.

5) Arise most nearly means STAND UP (d). Arise is similar in meaning to rise, but has a more dignified or poetic feeling to it. Here, the word suggests that the old mouse has a certain dignity or respect to him as he stands up to speak.

6) At the beginning of the story the Mice are looking for a way to "deal with" the Cat. Their minimum request is some way of knowing when the Cat might be close by: "some kind of early warning system that would tell them when the Cat was approaching."

7) The Cat is a problem because the mice are so afraid of her that their ordinary lives are severely disrupted: "the Mice were living in daily fear of the Cat's claws and hardly dared stir from their homes."

8) The mice respond with celebration to the young mouse's suggestion. They love it and are even amazed that no one came up with it before: "All the Mice were pleasantly surprised by the young Mouse's plan. No one could believe

that such a marvelous idea had not come up before."

9) The problem the old Mouse raises is that someone will have to hang a bell around the Cat's neck. In other words, someone will have to "bell the cat." Who will be able to do that and survive, since the Cat will presumably attack any mice that tried to accomplish this?

10) The young Mouse's plan is an example of saying something should be done: "All we have to do is hang a bell around the Cat's neck." Obviously, this idea would solve the problems the mice are having with the Cat. But actually being able to accomplish the task is something else entirely. It is not practical to focus on the advantages of the young mouse's plan before considering how that plan might actually be accomplished—or even if it is possible to be accomplished.

Thank you so much for reading this book. If you want to improve your English even more check out our

YouTube channel www.youtube.com/englishdanny

Facebook Page www.facebook.com/paperenglish

Website: www.dannyenglish.com

Made in United States
North Haven, CT
15 September 2023

41583424R10049